Changing Your Life Through Couponing........

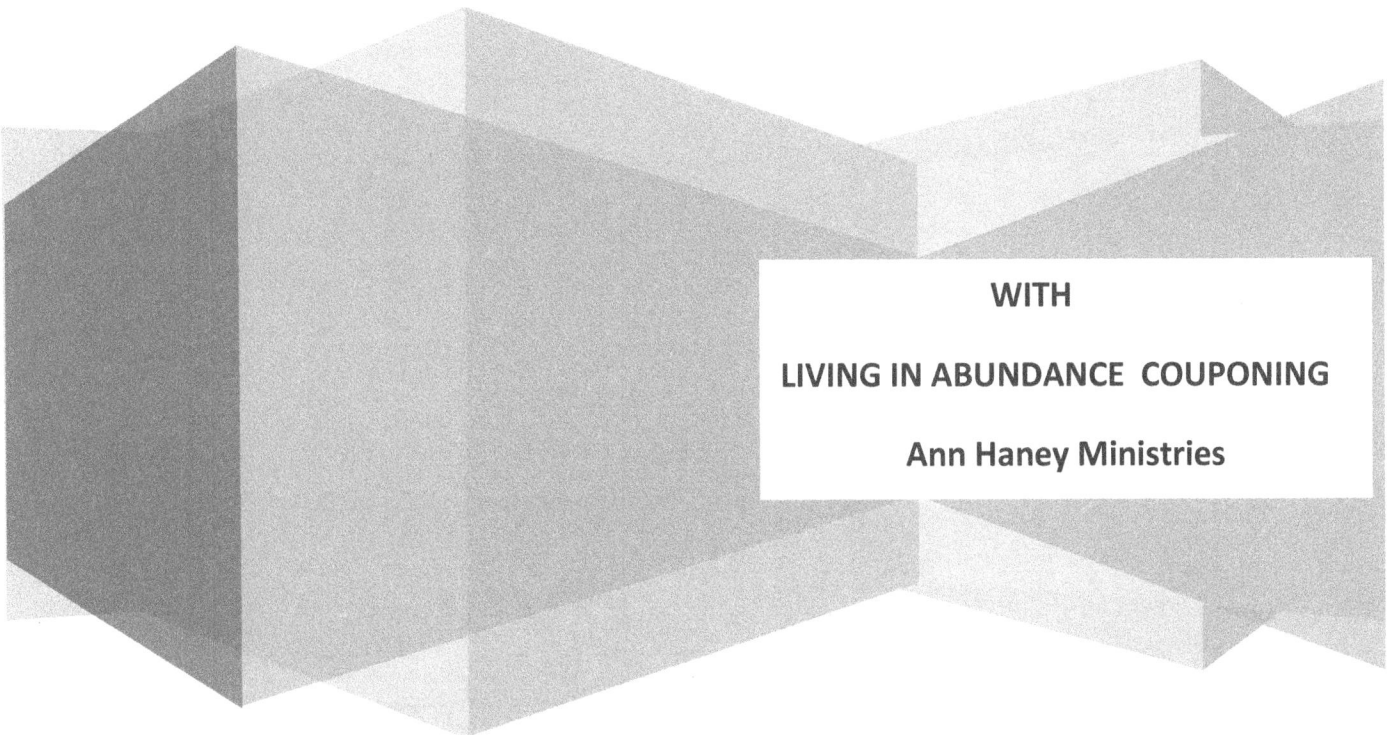

WITH

LIVING IN ABUNDANCE COUPONING

Ann Haney Ministries

Changing Your Life Through Couponing......

WITH

LIVING IN ABUNDANCE COUPONING

Ann Haney Ministries

Scripture taken from THE AMPLIFIED BIBLE, Old Testament

copyright © 1965, 1987 by the Zondervan Corporation.

THE MESSAGE BIBLE, Women of Faith

PUBLISHED BY AARON PUBLISHING

PO Box 1144

SHELBYVILLE, TN 37162

ISBN **978-0-9702265-8-7**

All pictures trademark of shown product.

PART 1

POLICY & PROCEDURE

MANUFACTURER/RETAILER/CONSUMER RELATIONSHIPS

STACKING FOR SUPER SAVINGS

DEALS THAT DELIVER DYNAMIC SAVINGS

Manufacturer/Retailer/Consumer Relationships......

Manufacturer—a business engaged in making something generally for the purpose of resell to a store

Retailer—a business which sells goods directly to the consumer

Consumer—a person who purchases goods

WHAT ARE THE BIBLICAL RESPONSIBILITIES OF MANUFACTURER/RETAILERS/CONSUMERS?

As a manufacturer/retailer God expects fair and honest business dealings. A business is generally a "for profit" organization, however, this does not mean manufacturers and retailers should excessively overprice their items putting hardship on the consumer. A fair price for a quality product is what's expected.

"God cares about honesty in the workplace; your business is HIS business."

Proverbs 16:11

As a consumer God expects us to treat businesses fairly as well, not trying to get over on them or misuse their policies to our benefit. We must remember we should treat others in the same manner we would want them to treat us if we owned the business. Our wealth will increase only when we put honest effort into it.

"Wealth obtained by fraud dwindles, but the one who gathers by labor INCREASES it."

Proverbs 13:11

Let's take a look at the 3 categories & their benefits:

1. Manufacturer---Produces the coupon for two reasons:
   1) Introduce a new product
   2) Increase sales of a product slump
      (many pay "slotting fees" for store shelf space & promote their product to keep it selling)

2. Retailer—Makes $.08 plus face value on every coupon redeemed PLUS the postage and handling to mail in the coupons.
3. Consumer—Rewarded with name brand products at drastically reduced prices, thus benefitting the overall economy of their households.

The goal of the manufacturer/retailer/consumer is to work together so that we all benefit from the efforts of one another. Each play an important part in prospering the economy and are responsible to do their part diligently.

Tips for working with the Manufacturer & Retailer for Less Stress & More Success.....

1. Know the store policy, ask if unsure
2. Buy balanced, limiting your purchases to 4 or less of like items
3. Be friendly
4. Make sure coupon matches item your purchasing
5. Do not switch peelies onto other products
6. Check expiration dates and do not use expired coupons
7. Give the cashier BOGO coupons with matching items last (they have to fill in the retail amount and won't have to hunt for it)
8. Divide up store coupons & manufacturer coupons (store coupons generally have to be hand-keyed in)
9. Be apologetic if you make an error
10. Do business as if you own the business
11. Operate wisely within the budget you have set, not overspending on unneeded items

Stacking for Super Savings......

Some stores allow stacking of a manufacturer coupon with a store or competitor coupon. For the stores where this is allowed you will find magnificent savings. REMEMBER: No store will allow you to stack two manufacturer on one item.

What is coupon stacking?

Using 1 Manufacturer coupon + 1 Store coupon on 1 item

What is the benefit of stacking? You will receive 2 discounts on 1 item for a really great deal!

What is super stacking?

Using 1 BOGO Manufacturer coupon with a Store BOGO sale

What is the benefit of super stacking? You will receive 100% discount at some drugstores (check with your local store) & 75% at some grocery stores. REMEMBER: At "allowing" stores where the first item rings up full price and the second one free—you can get 100% savings. At "allowing" stores where the items scan ½ price in a BOGO deal—you can get 75% savings. Many stores do this, so be sure and ask your local store if they do.

Store Policy Highlights......

WHAT COUPON DIFFERENCES YOU MIGHT SEE!

With the ever changing policies between different retailers, regions, and manufacturers, it is impossible to list the exact policy for each specific store. Below you will find a highlight of the different coupon acceptance terms I have seen across much of the United States.

STORE POLICIES HIGHLIGHTS........

- **Stack Manufacturer & Store Coupon at Many Stores**

- **Accept Scanable Internet Coupons**
  (Some limit # of like items ex. 1 or 2 "like")

- **Match Competitor Ads**
  (Some by word of mouth up to $10)

- **Accept Competitor Coupons**
  (Some will reject if it states "redeemable at"

- **Accept Competitor Catalina's Stating "manufacturer"**
  w/exp.

- **Coupon not to Exceed Item's Price at Some Stores**
  (Some stores mark the coupon down, others reject it)

- **Allow Overages**

- **On BOGO Deals**
  (Some allow coupon on both items)
  (Some require purchase of both --others scan ½ price)

- **Must Purchase Specified Sale Amount at Some Stores**
  (ex. 10/$10)

- **Ecoupons Do Not Double at Most Stores**

- **Ecoupons Do Not Stack at Most Stores**
  (Where allowed, neither will double)

- **Double $.50 or Less Everyday**
  (Some limit to the # of items that can be doubled ex. 2, 10)

- **Double $.50 or Less Everyday**
  (3 like items doubled 20 doubles per day)

- **Double $.60 or Less Everyday**
  (Some limit to 10 items)

- **Double Coupons Up to $.99**
  (3 like items doubled 20 doubles per day)

Sales That Add Up To Great Savings........

BOGO DEALS

MEGA DEALS

10/$10 DEALS

CATALINA DEALS

REWARD $ BACK DEALS

YOUR STORE POLICIES:

It is not important to know every specific policy for every store. Obviously a balanced couponer would not shop every store out there, but would choose a few to capture the best bargains. I would suggest every couponer find out their specific store policy. The best way to do this is to ask the store manager from YOUR store what he/she does or does not allow. They should be happy to oblige you with this information as they see your willingness to work within their store guidelines.

Below you will find worksheets for recording specific store information. List these as bullet points to remind you of their policies.

STORE:_____

(Check the items which apply & use the bullet points for special restrictions that apply)

COUPONS ACCEPTED: Manufacturer _____   Store_____   Competitor _____

● ————————————————————————————————

STACKING: _____ Yes   _____No

● ————————————————————————————————

LIMIT ON STACKING: _____Yes   _____No

- ––

ECOUPON ACCEPTANCE: _____Yes _____No

- ––

INTERNET COUPONS: _____Yes _____No

- ––

COMPETITOR ADS: _____Yes _____No

- ––

DOUBLE COUPONS: _____Yes _____No

- ––

RAIN CHECKS: _____Yes _____No

- ––

SALE SUBSTITUTIONS: _____Yes _____No

- ––

OVERAGES: _____Yes _____No

- ––

CATALINA'S: _____Yes _____No

- ––

BOGO DEAL LIMIT: _____Yes _____No

- ––

BOGO COUPON ACCEPTANCE: _____Yes _____No

- ––

SALE BEGINNING/ENDING DAY:

- ––

EXTRA RESTRICTIONS OR GUIDELINES:

- _____
- _____
- _____
- _____

STORE:_____

(Check the items which apply & use the bullet points for special restrictions that apply)

COUPONS ACCEPTED: Manufacturer _____   Store_____   Competitor _____

- _____

STACKING: _____ Yes   _____No

- _____

LIMIT ON STACKING: _____Yes   _____No

- _____

ECOUPON ACCEPTANCE: _____Yes   _____No

- _____

INTERNET COUPONS: _____Yes _____No

- _____

COMPETITOR ADS: _____Yes _____No

- _____

DOUBLE COUPONS: _____Yes _____No

- _____

RAIN CHECKS: _____Yes _____No

- _____

SALE SUBSTITUTIONS: _____Yes _____No

- ————————————————————————————————

OVERAGES: _____Yes _____No

- ————————————————————————————————

CATALINA'S: _____Yes _____No

- ————————————————————————————————

BOGO DEAL LIMIT: _____Yes _____No

- ————————————————————————————————

BOGO COUPON ACCEPTANCE: _____Yes _____No

- ————————————————————————————————

SALE BEGINNING/ENDING DAY:

- ————————————————————————————————

EXTRA RESTRICTIONS OR GUIDELINES:

- ————————————————————————————————
- ————————————————————————————————
- ————————————————————————————————
- ————————————————————————————————

STORE:_____

(Check the items which apply & use the bullet points for special restrictions that apply)

COUPONS ACCEPTED: Manufacturer _____   Store_____   Competitor _____

- ————————————————————————————————

STACKING: _____ Yes _____No

- ———————————————————————————

LIMIT ON STACKING: _____Yes   _____No

- ———————————————————————————

ECOUPON ACCEPTANCE: _____Yes   _____No

- ———————————————————————————

INTERNET COUPONS: _____Yes _____No

- ———————————————————————————

COMPETITOR ADS: _____Yes _____No

- ———————————————————————————

DOUBLE COUPONS: _____Yes _____No

- ———————————————————————————

RAIN CHECKS: _____Yes _____No

- ———————————————————————————

SALE SUBSTITUTIONS: _____Yes _____No

- ———————————————————————————

OVERAGES: _____Yes _____No

- ———————————————————————————

CATALINA'S: _____Yes _____No

- ———————————————————————————

BOGO DEAL LIMIT: _____Yes _____No

- ———————————————————————————

BOGO COUPON ACCEPTANCE: _____Yes _____No

- ———————————————————————————

SALE BEGINNING/ENDING DAY:

- _____

EXTRA RESTRICTIONS OR GUIDELINES:

- _____
- _____
- _____
- _____

STORE:_____

(Check the items which apply & use the bullet points for special restrictions that apply)

COUPONS ACCEPTED: Manufacturer _____   Store_____   Competitor _____

- _____

STACKING: _____ Yes   _____No

- _____

LIMIT ON STACKING: _____Yes   _____No

- _____

ECOUPON ACCEPTANCE: _____Yes   _____No

- _____

INTERNET COUPONS: _____Yes _____No

- _____

COMPETITOR ADS: _____Yes   _____No

- _____

DOUBLE COUPONS: _____Yes   _____No

- ─────────────────────────────────

RAIN CHECKS: _____Yes _____No

- ─────────────────────────────────

SALE SUBSTITUTIONS: _____Yes _____No

- ─────────────────────────────────

OVERAGES: _____Yes _____No

- ─────────────────────────────────

CATALINA'S: _____Yes _____No

- ─────────────────────────────────

BOGO DEAL LIMIT: _____Yes _____No

- ─────────────────────────────────

BOGO COUPON ACCEPTANCE: _____Yes _____No

- ─────────────────────────────────

SALE BEGINNING/ENDING DAY:

- ─────────────────────────────────

EXTRA RESTRICTIONS OR GUIDELINES:

- ─────────────────────────────────
- ─────────────────────────────────
- ─────────────────────────────────
- ─────────────────────────────────

STORE:_____

(Check the items which apply & use the bullet points for special restrictions that apply)

COUPONS ACCEPTED: Manufacturer _____   Store_____   Competitor _____

● ————————————————————————————————————

STACKING: _____ Yes   _____No

● ————————————————————————————————————

LIMIT ON STACKING: _____Yes   _____No

● ————————————————————————————————————

ECOUPON ACCEPTANCE: _____Yes   _____No

● ————————————————————————————————————

INTERNET COUPONS: _____Yes _____No

● ————————————————————————————————————

COMPETITOR ADS: _____Yes   _____No

● ————————————————————————————————————

DOUBLE COUPONS: _____Yes   _____No

● ————————————————————————————————————

RAIN CHECKS: _____Yes _____No

● ————————————————————————————————————

SALE SUBSTITUTIONS: _____Yes   _____No

● ————————————————————————————————————

OVERAGES: _____Yes   _____No

● ————————————————————————————————————

CATALINA'S: _____Yes   _____No

● ————————————————————————————————————

BOGO DEAL LIMIT: _____Yes   _____No

● ————————————————————————————————————

BOGO COUPON ACCEPTANCE: _____Yes _____No

● ——

SALE BEGINNING/ENDING DAY:

● ——

EXTRA RESTRICTIONS OR GUIDELINES:

● ——

● ——

● ——

● ——

STORE:_____

(Check the items which apply & use the bullet points for special restrictions that apply)

COUPONS ACCEPTED: Manufacturer _____   Store_____   Competitor _____

● ——

STACKING: _____ Yes _____No

● ——

LIMIT ON STACKING: _____Yes _____No

● ——

ECOUPON ACCEPTANCE: _____Yes _____No

● ——

INTERNET COUPONS: _____Yes _____No

● ——

COMPETITOR ADS: _____Yes _____No

- ——————————————————————————————

DOUBLE COUPONS: _____Yes _____No

- ——————————————————————————————

RAIN CHECKS: _____Yes _____No

- ——————————————————————————————

SALE SUBSTITUTIONS: _____Yes _____No

- ——————————————————————————————

OVERAGES: _____Yes _____No

- ——————————————————————————————

CATALINA'S: _____Yes _____No

- ——————————————————————————————

BOGO DEAL LIMIT: _____Yes _____No

- ——————————————————————————————

BOGO COUPON ACCEPTANCE: _____Yes _____No

- ——————————————————————————————

SALE BEGINNING/ENDING DAY:

- ——————————————————————————————

EXTRA RESTRICTIONS OR GUIDELINES:

- ——————————————————————————————
- ——————————————————————————————
- ——————————————————————————————
- ——————————————————————————————

PART 1 REVIEW

"POLICY & PROCEDURE"

Sample the Savings!

Directions: Create a deal for each scenario using the coupons/products/sale below.

SALE: BOGO—reg. price $3.99   MANUFACTURER COUPON: Face Value---$.75

Store 1---POLICY states BOGO may purchase 1, Coupon doubles face value up to $.99

What will you pay for this item?

Reg. Price---

BOGO discount---

Coupon discount----

Final Cost on 1----

SALE: BOGO—reg. price $1.59   MANUFACTURER COUPON: Face Value---$.50/2

STORE COUPON: Face Value---$.50/2

Store 2---POLICY states BOGO may purchase 1, Coupon doubles face value up to $.50, Can Stack Manufacturer + Store Coupon

What will you pay for this item?

Reg. Price---

BOGO discount---

Coupon discount----

Final Cost on 1----

SALE: MEGA $4/4 —reg. price $5.99   MANUF. COUPON: Face Value---(2) BOGO

MANUF. COUPON: Face Value---(2) $.75

Store 3: Must buy 4 to get $4 OFF, No limit on like coupons

What will you pay for this item?

Reg. Price---

Coupon discount----

Final Cost on 1----

SALE: Comp. AD for $1 each   MANUF. COUPON: Face Value---$.75/3

STORE COUPON: FACE VALUE--- Buy 2 get 1 Free

Store 4: Match Comp. Ad, No doubling, Stack Manufacturer + Store Coupon

What will you pay for this item?

Reg. Price---

Coupon discount----

Final Cost on 1----

SALE: BOGO---Reg. Price $6.29   MANUF. COUPON: Face Value---$.3.00

COMP. COUPON: FACE VALUE---$1.00

Store 5: Stack Manuf. + Store Coupon, Allow Overages, Accept Comp. Coupon

What will you pay for this item?

Reg. Price---

BOGO discount---

Coupon discount----

Final Cost on 1----

HOW DID YOU DO?

Some possible solutions to these scenarios are as follows:

Store 1---You will pay --$.50

Reg. Price--$3.99

BOGO discount—$1.99

Coupon discount--$1.50

Final Cost--$.50

Store 2---You will pay --$.09

Reg. Price--$1.59

BOGO discount—will remain $1.59 because we must purchase 2 to abide by coupon specifications.

Coupon discount--$1.50

Final Cost--$.09

Store 3---You will pay --$6.48/4

Reg. Price--$5.99

Coupon discount--$1.50 + $11.98 for BOGO's +$4 MEGA TOTAL DISCOUNT: $17.48

Final Cost--$1.62 each

Store 4---You will pay --$1.25/3

Reg. Price--$1.00

Coupon discount--$.75/3 man +B2G1 (buy 2 get 1) TOTAL DISCOUNT: $1.75

Final Cost--$.42 each

Store 5---You will pay --nothing

Reg. Price--$6.29

BOGO discount—$3.15

Coupon discount--$4.00

Final Cost--$.85 OVERAGE

THESE ARE ALL SAMPLE DEALS FOR SAMPLE STORES. SOME EXAMPLES CAN BE APPLIED TO OTHER STORES AS WELL. THE STORE POLICIES IN THIS BOOK ARE A GENERAL GUIDELINE AND NOT INTENDED TO BE THE EXACT POLICY FOR EACH STORE. DIFFERENT REGIONS POLICIES OFTEN VARY, HOWEVER THIS IS A GOOD SAMPLING OF ALMOST EVERY TYPE OF SCENARIO OF

COUPONING POLICIES YOU WILL PROBABLY ENCOUNTER. ALWAYS ASK THE STORE FOR SPECIFIC GUIDELINES PERTAINING TO THEM INDIVIDUALLY.

ACTION & ANSWER MATCH UP…..

Directions: Match the proper response to the scripture which best fits.

Action---

1. _____Know the store policy, ask if unsure
2. _____Buy balanced, limiting your purchases to 4 or less of like items
3. _____Be friendly
4. _____Make sure coupon matches item purchasing
5. _____Do not switch peelies onto other products
6. _____Check expiration dates and do not use expired coupons
7. _____Give the cashier BOGO coupons with matching items last (they have to fill in the retail and won't have to hunt for it)
8. _____Divide up store coupons & manufacturer coupons (store coupons generally have to be hand-keyed in)
9. _____Be apologetic if you make an error
10. _____Do business as if you own the business
11. _____Operate wisely within the budget you have set, not overspending on unneeded items

Answer---

A. "For which of you, intending to build a tower, does not sit down first and count the cost, whether he may have enough to finish it;….." Luke 14:28
B. "Wealth obtained by fraud dwindles, but the one who gathers by labor increases it." Proverbs 13:11
C. "Woe to him who builds his house WITHOUT righteousness….." Jeremiah 22:13
D. "Look! The wages you failed to pay the workmen who mowed your fields are crying out against you. The cries of the harvesters have reached the ears of the Lord Almighty." James 5:4
E. "….He loves it when business is aboveboard." Proverbs 11:1
F. "What is desirable in a person is kindness…" Proverbs 19:22
G. "My people perish from lack of knowledge…" Hosea 4:6

H. "Protect yourself against the least bit of greed. Life is not defined by what you have, even when you have a lot." Luke 12:15
I. "Humility and fear of the Lord bring wealth, honor, and life." Proverbs 22:4
J. "Let each of you not only look to his own interests but also to the interests of others." Philippians 2:4
K. "Contribute to the needs of the saints and seek to show hospitality." Romans 12:13

HOW DID YOU DO?

Answers to the above may vary and many scriptures could refer to the same scenario. The important thing to note here is that everything in life pertains to a relevant instruction from God's word, telling us how we should live to obtain favor and blessing.

Answer Key:

1. G   2. H   3. F   4. D   5. B   6. C   7. K   8. J   9. I   10. E   11. A

PART 2

COUPON SOURCES

SAFE SITES FOR ULTIMATE SAVINGS

COUPON SOURCES WITHOUT THE INTERNET

SMART PHONE APPS THAT BUILD SAVINGS

"People Perish for Lack of Knowledge....." Hosea 4:6

NOT LACK OF RESOURCES!!!!

I am a firm believer that everything we need to be successful in this lifetime has already been provided for us. The resources are there; we must uncover them to discover the abundance that awaits us. But, how do we get this wisdom you may be wondering? Let me give you a few key tips that will help put you on your way to uncovering the hidden treasures that await you.

1. Ask for wisdom
   *James 1:5 "If any of you lack **wisdom**, let him ask of **God**, that **gives** to all men liberally..."*

   Ask God for wisdom pertaining to your circumstances. He will prompt you in an area to look into.

2. Uncover truths that will conquer your situation
   *Psalm 119:130 "The unfolding of your words gives **light**; it gives understanding to the simple."*

   Use the wisdom God gives you to understand what you need to know to change your circumstances.

3. Seek counsel
   Proverbs 15:22 "Without consultation, plans are frustrated, but with many counselors they succeed."

   Ask for advice from those who are trusted and successful in the area you want to be.

4. Research the Principles to make sure they are profitable
   *1 Thessalonians 5:21 "**Test all things**, and hold firmly that which is good."*

   Check the past track record of the success of what you are attempting to do. Has it been a profitable endeavor for others? If so, what did they do to make it profitable OR if not what can be learned from the past mistakes of this endeavor.

5. Apply the Knowledge Learned
   James 1:22 "Be ye doers of the word and not only hearers..."

Knowledge will never transpire into success if it is not applied.

Safe Sites for Ultimate Savings....

Find coupon blog sites for your area. What is a blog site? Simply stated a blog site is a site based around a specific interest that gives people all the details pertaining to that topic. A coupon blog site will give couponers the following information:

1. Local Store Sales
2. Best Buys
3. Printable Coupon Links
4. Ecoupon Links
5. Unadvertised Deals
6. Sale Previews
7. Store Policies
8. Coupon Match-Ups
9. Coupon Tips
10. Organizational Ideas

Google search "coupon blog sites "your state" to locate the closest one in your area. Same stores may vary in sales according to the region they are located in, so it is important to try and find one closest to your area.

When using the internet as a resource for finding coupons you will see many different abbreviations in regard to couponing. Couponing has a language all its own and it's necessary to know what these abbreviations mean to get the most out of your internet experience. Facebook is another good place to find coupons. "Like" the product's on Facebook you want coupons for and you will have access to coupons through their site.

COUPON LINGO...

Q--coupon	DND--do not double
SS--smart source coupon	FAR--free after rebate
RP--red plum coupon	HBA--health and beauty aids
RR--register rewards	IVC--instant value coupon (Wal-Green's)
ECB--extra cash back	IP--internet printable
SCR--single cash rebates	MIR--mail in rebate
+UP-- Rite-Aid Reward	POP--proof of purchase
PG--proctor and gamble coupon	UPC--universal product code
FL--Food Lion coupon	NED--no expiration date
wyb--when you buy	BTFE--box tops for education
BOGO--buy one get one free	CAT--Catalina
POP--proof of purchase	BOGO1/2--buy one get one half off
OOP--out of pocket expense	YMMV-- your mileage may vary
FLIPS-Food Lion internet printables	

The internet is a fantastic tool to use to find those coupons for great discounts. Where do you look? Below are some sites for different coupons to maximize your savings. Always set up a coupon email for registering on these sites, do not use your main email account. Download the coupon driver for formatted scanable coupons.

INTERNET PRINTABLE COUPONS

smartsource.com

coupon.com

eatbetteramerica.com

slickdeals.com

save-a-lot.com (manuf & store)

healthesavers.com

organicvalley.coop

couponnetwork.com

wholefoodsmarket.com

healthsavers.com (diabetic)

restaurant.com (gift certificates)

redplum.com

earthfare.com

target.com

foodlion.com

snackpicks.com

pillsbury.com

bettycrocker.com

recyclebank.com

Ecoupons are another great way to save money, especially if you can't find a paper coupon for a product. What are ecoupons? Ecoupons are digital coupons you load to your loyalty shopper cards for an instant discount upon scanning of item and shopper's card. Some ecoupons that you load to your loyalty card, however are deposited to an account for you by which you can draw out your savings up to 4 times a year. For example, the last two on the list below will deposit the savings you loaded to your account and accumulate until you request your check.

Let's look at an example of how this works:

You load a $.50 coupon to your card, purchase the item, the $.50 is put in a savings account until you determine to draw it out. Your account can be accessed at these sites to see your balance.

Some ecoupon tips to remember:

1. Most do not double
2. Most do not stack with another coupon (check individual store policy)
3. Most will come off item only once, even if you buy 2 items
4. All expire
5. Most limit the number that can be added to the loyalty card

E COUPONS

cellfire.com /Kroger card
shortcuts.com / Kroger card
krogers.com /Kroger card
pgesaver.com / Kroger card
foodlion.com / Food Lion card
harristeeter.com /load to HT card
upromise.com /savings deposited to account
savingstar.com /savings deposited to account

Even though the internet is a great resource, it can often times frustrate you when your coupons do not print. There are a couple of things you should know when you encounter such a problem. Below I have listed these things and given you possible solutions to remedy the problem.

PRINTER PROBLEMS....

1. **Change Browsers (ex. Firefox, Internet Explorer, Safari, etc....**
   NOTE: WHICHEVER BROWSER THE COUPON LINK WAS CREATED IN MUST USE THE SAME BROWSER TO PRINT

Example:
http://bricks.coupons.com/Start.aspt59687503&bt=wg&o=53740&ci=1&cJAY

BROWSER CODES:
Firefox ---- "wg" or "vg"
Internet Explorer ---- "wi" or "vi"
Safari---- "xs"

2. **Check Security Settings (may need to change these to allow)**

Coupon Sources Without The Internet.....

There are many resources you can use without getting caught up in the world of internet. Let's look at some of these sources:

1. Blinkies (Smart Source machines located in stores that signal you with a flashing light and prompt you to pull out a coupon)
   These are manufacturer coupons

2. Peelies (Manufacturer coupons that offer instant rebates on the product it is attached to) Do not put these on other products or use them with another manufacturer coupon

3. Catalina's (Manufacturer coupons that are given upon checkout based either upon your buying habits or purchase of required items) You can find out current Catalina's by going to couponnetwork.com.

4. Tear Pads (Manufacturer coupons placed near the product specified on a type of note pad)

5. Magazines (Many magazines have manufacturer coupons for a variety of products that rotate within the 6-8 week sale cycle)

6. Store/Pharmacy Coupons (These are usually located at the store service desk, pharmacy counters, or by the store weekly ads. Be alert some are often manufacturer coupons)

7. Sunday Newspaper (This is your largest resource for free standing coupons! It will often have store coupons inside as well as the weekly manufacturer coupons) Generally no coupon inserts will appear on a holiday weekend or the fifth Sunday of the month with the exception of Proctor & Gamble upon occasion. Always buy at least 2 newspapers. Some stores will discount the Sunday paper Monday morning.

8. Contact Manufacturer directly

Smart Phone Apps that Build Savings.....

With technology ever-changing, we are seeing more and more ways to apply savings. Smart phone apps are definitely one of them. Simply stated it is an application you download on your smart phone through the "app store" (already on your phone) that will allow you savings in many different areas. Here are a few:

1. Hotel Savings (allows you to locate the cheapest hotel by area)
2. Gas Savings (allows you to locate the cheapest place to buy gas)
3. % Calculators (calculate instant % off the price of merchandise quickly)
4. Tax Calculators (allows you to know the total, just put in your tax %)
5. Barcode Scanners (allows you to scan an item and shows you the cheapest place to buy)
6. Shopping (list maker, coupon deducter, tax adder—a complete shopper's experience)
7. Store Coupon (instant codes to show the cashier for immediate discounts at many retail stores/restaurants/services)

Keeping those apps running smoothly on your phone with the following tips:

1. Download updates whenever your phone prompts you to.
2. Power off your phone occasionally for less jam ups
3. Search out the "free" apps
4. Read app reviews
5. Remove any apps you don't use or like to free up phone and speed up functionality

Favorite Blog Sites:

- _____
- _____
- _____
- _____

Favorite Printable Coupon Sites:

- _____
- _____
- _____
- _____
- _____
- _____
- _____
- _____

Favorite Phone Apps:

- _____
- _____
- _____
- _____

PART 2 REVIEW

"COUPON SOURCES"

Lingo Match-Up!

Directions: Match the correct abbreviation with the proper word or group of words.

A. Coupon	_____ HBA	
B. Out of Pocket	_____ FL	
C. Red Plum	_____ BOGO 1/2	
D. Smart Source	_____ +UP	
E. Food Lion Internet Printables	_____ SS	
F. Food Lion	_____ OOP	
G. Proctor & Gamble	_____ DND	
H. Register Rewards	_____ CAT	
I. Up Rewards	_____ POP	
J. Single Check Rebate	_____ ECB	
K. Extra Cash Back	_____ RR	
L. When You Buy	_____ FLIP	
M. Buy One Get One Free	_____ MIR	
N. Buy One Get One Half	_____ IP	
O. Free After Rebate	_____ FAR	
P. Proof of Purchase	_____ WYB	
Q. When You Buy	_____ RP	
R. Health and Beauty Aids	_____ IVC	
S. Instant Value Coupon	_____ BOGO	
T. Internet Printable	_____ UPC	
U. Mail In Rebate	_____ NED	
V. Universal Product Code	_____ CAT	
W. No Expiration Date	_____ YMMV	
X. Box Tops For Education	_____ PG	
Y. Catalina	_____ Q	
Z. Your Mileage May Vary	_____ BTFE	
AA. Do Not Double	_____ SCR	

HOW DID YOU DO?

Answer Key:

R-F-N-I-D-B-AA-Y-P-K-H-E-U-T-O-Q-C-S-M-V-W-Y-Z-G-A-X-J

TRUE OR FALSE!

Directions: Place T or F beside the statement indicating if it is true or false.

1. _____ Ecoupons double
2. _____ Most blog sites do coupon matchups with sales
3. _____ Coupon Internet sites allow 2 prints per computer
4. _____ Use your main email account for registering with coupon sites
5. _____ Trouble printing a coupon is generally a browser or security setting problem.
6. _____ Ecoupons are manufacturer coupons
7. _____ You can use an ecoupon on more than 1 item.
8. _____ Some online rebate programs pay percentages for online purchases
9. _____ Companies can be emailed directly to receive coupons
10. _____ Catalina's are store coupons
11. _____ Blinkie coupons should be filed until the item goes on sale
12. _____ You should only buy 1 Sunday newspaper
13. _____ Sunday papers have only manufacturer coupons inside
14. _____ Some stores discount the Sunday papers left on Monday's
15. _____ You can find out the Catalina deals offered in advance
16. _____ Never download updates to smart phone apps
17. _____ Smart phone apps can be instantly deducted using code on phone by the cashier
18. _____ Search for "free" smart phone apps before paying for an app
19. _____ Locate blog sites for your area to see local deals
20. _____ A browser code cannot be changed to allow coupons to print

HOW DID YOU DO?

1. F	2. T	3. T	4. F	5. T	6. T	7. F	8. T	9. T	10. F	11. T	12. F
12. F		14. T	15. T	16. F	17. T	18. T	19. T	20. F			

PART 3

ORGANIZING & STOCKPILING

CLIPPING WITHOUT CLUTTER

STEPS TO BUILDING A BALANCED STOCKPILE

PREPARING, PLANNING, & CONQUERING

Clipping Without Clutter....

The big question that usually arises is "Do I have to clip all those coupons?" The answer is "NO". However, there are some basic tips to knowing exactly what you should cut and what you should not.

You should clip coupons for:

       Repetitive Sale Items

       Frequently Used Items

       Money Maker Items

You should clip coupons:

       Weekly when you get the Sunday paper

       Whenever new coupon booklets come in the mail or you pick up from the store

       When you are at appointments where all you can do is wait (dr, dentist, sports practices, etc...)

You should print coupons:

       When alerted by email

       When you prepare your list

       At least every 2 weeks

Organizing Coupons....

1. File coupons in 9 pocket baseball card holder pouches in a 1 ½" 3 ring binder separated by dividers
2. Break down categories into specifics (ex. Instead of personal hygiene make categories for soaps, shampoos, razors, etc...)

3. Write your list on shopping templates as shown in the part 3 video or see get them on my website livinginabundacecouponing.com (this keeps you from overspending, forgetting your rain checks and balancing your stockpile)
4. Pull coupons to use and place in expandable pouch for search –free shopping
5. Put coupons for items placed in cart in front of the pouch so you can hand them directly to the cashier without having to sort through the ones for the items they were out of.
6. Paper clip rain checks to coupons and leave in the pouch for your next shopping trip.
7. Pull expired coupons at the beginning of each month

Steps to Building A Balanced Stockpile….

In order to understand the importance of this we must look to the ant.

"The ant…without having any chief, officer or ruler, prepares her bread in summer and gathers her food in harvest."

Proverbs 6:6-8

The ant is one of the wisest creatures there is. It knows the need for a stockpile and wastes no time in building it. The ant works when the harvest is ready. We too must use wisdom and buy when the sales present themselves and prepare for the time when sales are slim. Everything is seasonal. We will see times when prices rise and times when they fall and we must be prepared for the times of need. We can never be assured of what tomorrow brings, but we can be assured that God who knows tomorrow gives us wisdom for today to be ready come what may. We can be ready for pay cuts, lose of employment, inflation, natural disasters and anything that might come our way.

The stockpile is your key to success in couponing. Keep it built and fear diminishes. Let is lapse and you must start again.

7 Steps to Building a Balanced Stockpile:

1. Make a list of commonly used items
2. Determine number needed for 6-8 week sale cycle
3. Add a few to this number for unexpected needs
4. Place food items soonest to expire in front
5. Buy only the number needed to reach stockpile quota
6. Stock all like items together (hygiene items, cleaning items, can goods, etc…)
7. Divide meat in family size portions and freeze

In order to stay on top of your stockpile you will need to do the following:

1. Allot a weekly budget designated just for adding to your stockpile
2. Choose those items which are on sale with coupons
3. Watch for closeouts
4. Date freezer items
5. Watch for expiring deals
6. Don't ever stop building

"The plans of the diligent lead surely to ABUNDANCE..."

Proverbs 21:5

Preparing, Planning & Conquering.....

To be a conquer we must remember this one key fact----

"I can do ALL THINGS through Christ who strengthens me."

Philippians 4:13

Once we have understood AND believe this fact the victory is assured! Here are a few more tips for becoming that conqueror:

1. Keep a weekly needs list for repetitive needs
2. Set a budget for your needs list AND stick to it
3. Buy as many of the needed items as possible with coupons
4. Look for profit items to lower cost of needs
5. Make list prior to going to the store
6. Take your binder in the car for unadvertised deals
7. Plan early don't wait till the last day of the sale (the early bird gets the worm)
8. Don't use savings to overindulge in spending

My commonly needed items/stockpile quota:

● ——————————————— ——— ● ——————————————— ———

- ——————————— —
- ——————————— ——
- ——————————— ——
- ——————————— ——
- ——————————— ——
- ——————————— ——
- ——————————— ——
- ——————————— —
- ——————————— ——
- ——————————— ——
- ——————————— ——
- ——————————— ——
- ——————————— ——
- ——————————— ——

- ——————————— ——
- ——————————— ——
- ——————————— ——
- ——————————— ——
- ——————————— ——
- ——————————— ——
- ——————————— ——
- ——————————— ——
- ——————————— ——
- ——————————— ——
- ——————————— ——
- ——————————— ——
- ——————————— ——
- ——————————— ——

My Binder Categories:

- ———————————
- ———————————
- ———————————
- ———————————
- ———————————
- ———————————
- ———————————
- ———————————

- _____
- _____
- _____
- _____
- _____
- _____
- _____
- _____
- _____
- _____
- _____
- _____
- _____
- _____
- _____

My Weekly Stockpile Budget: _____

My Weekly Needs Budget: _____

PART 3 REVIEW

"ORGANIZING & STOCKPILING"

DO AND DON'T MATCH-UP!

Directions: Place the correct statement in the appropriate column.

1. Use your savings for an extra wanted item
2. Print all coupons for all items offered
3. Plan a stockpile budget
4. Wait till the last day of the sale to shop
5. Clip all coupons from the Sunday paper
6. Cut coupons at doctors and dentists appointments or sporting practices
7. Breakdown categories within binders into specifics
8. Pull your coupons in the store when you see the item is on sale
9. Pull expired coupons at the beginning of the month
10. Buy only the # of items needed to reach stockpile quota set
11. Make your list while shopping to assure you don't miss something
12. Put rain checks in binders
13. Wait till your stockpile is low to rebuild
14. Buy items that are on sale with a coupon to rebuild stockpile

DO	DON'T
_____	_____
_____	_____
_____	_____
_____	_____
_____	_____
_____	_____
_____	_____

HOW DID YOU DO?

Answer Key:

DO's—3, 6, 7, 9, 10, 14

DON'T's—1,2,4,5,8,11,12,13

PART 4

DRUG STORE DEALING

MAKING SENSE OF REWARD PROGRAMS

TURNING NEED INTO FREEBIES

ROLLING REWARD FOR MINIMAL COST

Making Sense of Reward Programs.....

Drug stores are what I like to call the "College of Couponing". Basic grocery stores offer us the opportunity to gradually learn the couponing principles on a somewhat smaller and less complicated scale than drug stores. However, once we successfully accomplish these stores it is time to push out into the deep and move on the college. In part 4 we are going to:

"Push out into the deep and let down our nets for a catch."

Luke 5:4

And when you do this you will claim this statement:

"They were amazed at the haul of fish they had made."

Luke 5:9

Your key to success in working with the drug stores is to remember you don't have to start with all the answers, just start. Start by working 1 small deal until you achieve confidence and are ready to tackle a bigger deal. Allow yourself mistakes! No one is a perfect, we all make mistakes, even the so called "pros". The important thing is you don't quit and you're not afraid to step out into the unknown. The greatest treasuries are those we often have to wade out into the deep to find. Take your time and enjoy your couponing venture. Slow and steady makes right and ready in couponing.

".....he who hurries his footsteps errs."

Proverbs 19:2

&

"A bonanza at the beginning is no guarantee of a blessing at the end."

Proverbs 20:21

Let's take a look into the policies of 3 well-known drug stores. Let me note that each policy is just a basic guideline and all are contingent upon local store restrictions.

WALGREEN'S

Policy:

1. Manufacturer + Store Ad Coupon + IVC (instant value coupon) may be stacked on 1 item

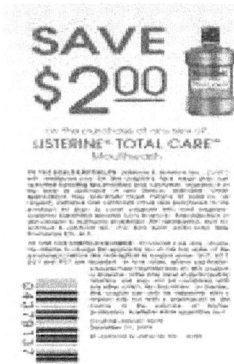

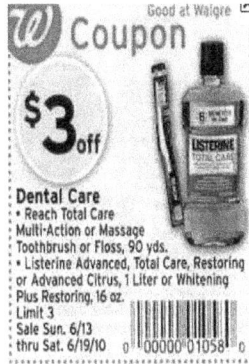

2. May purchase 1 sale item UNLESS it is a BOGO
3. Rain Checks are not usually issued on RR items
4. BOGO Sales accept coupons on both items
5. RR counts as a coupon
6. BOGO sale can be stacked with a BOGO coupon for 2 FREE

Tips for shopping Walgreen's:

1. Do multiple deals in different transactions
2. RR usually expire two weeks from purchase date
3. RR is determined prior to coupon deduction
   Ex. $8 PG purchase states receive $2 RR---OOP may be $6 after $2 coupon (will still receive the $2 RR
4. RR are reimbursed from the manufacturer to the store
5. Rain checks do not expire

What is a RR?

Simply stated it is a Catalina you are given when making a required purchase that has cash value. For instance a $2 RR is worth $2 cash towards a purchase of a different item. NOTE: Do not use a RR to pay for another item like the one you received the RR from purchasing. To do so would result in not receiving another RR. The RR can be used on any different item within the store with a few exceptions (tobacco, prescriptions, etc..... see store for specifics.) These print out separately from the receipt.

EXAMPLE OF RR SALE ITEM:

EXAMPLE OF RR:

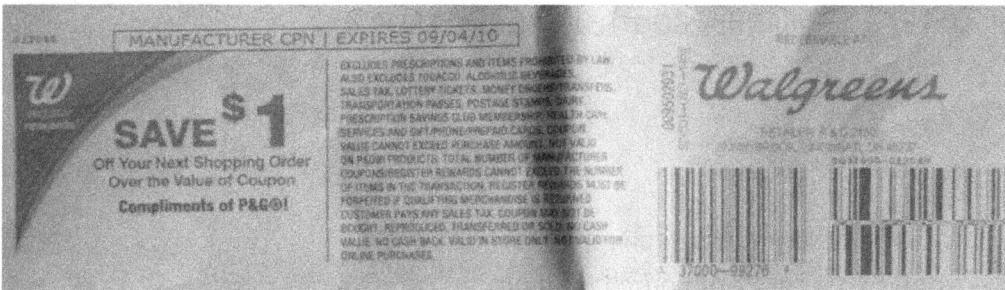

At Walgreen's you may never have more coupons than items. It may be necessary at times to purchase what is known as a filler item to even out your coupon/item count.

For example: Purchase 1 Finish Detergent

Apply (1) manuf coupo + (1) store ad coupon

Pay with (1) RR (which counts as a coupon)

Summary: You will need to buy 2 filler items so that your coupon count will equal your items. A filler may be any item in the store. Check clearance for cheap items or buy a carmel as filler.

NOTE: IVC coupons count as 1 no matter how many of the items you buy. The discount will come off the appropriate # of items but will only count as one. Likewise, store ad coupons work exactly the same way.

CVS

Policy:

1. Manufacturer +Store CRT + ECB may be stacked together on 1 item

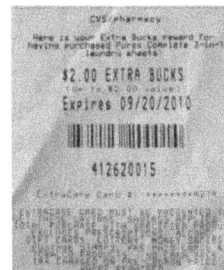

2. May purchase 1 sale item UNLESS it is a BOGO
3. Rain checks are issued on out of stock ECB items
4. On a BOGO sale coupons will be accepted on both items
5. 2% is given back in ECB's quarterly
6. BOGO sale can be stacked with a BOGO coupon for 2 items FREE
7. Limit the # you can buy on ECB items

Tips for shopping CVS:

1. CVS honors competitor RX coupons (ex. Gift cards, etc...)
2. CVS will refund CVS brand or cosmetic purchase opened or unopened with a receipt
3. ECB's expire in 4 weeks/CRT's expire in 2 weeks
4. No ECB's allowed on RX, alcohol, tobacco, lottery, stamps, giftcards, money orders, prepaid debit cards
5. Rain checks do not expire
6. Scan CVS card at in store scanner for instant coupons
7. Give coupons in this order: $ off $, CRT's, Manuf, ECB's

RITEAID

Policy:

1. Manufacturer Coupon + Store Ad Coupon + UP Reward may be stacked on 1 item

2. May purchase 1 sale item UNLESS it is a BOGO
3. Rain checks are issued on +UP reward & SCR items
4. On a BOGO sale coupons will be accepted on both items.
5. SCR's will be issued on out of stock items that a rain check was issued for after the rebate period . SCR's are $ rewards issued for specific items monthly. The reward's are paid by a check mailed to you at the end of the month. Ask them to issue your check at the end of the month or you will not receive all the rebates back. You do this online on their website.

Tips for shopping Rite Aid:

1. Enter receipts for SCR items @ riteaidrebateplus.com
2. Request your check for SCR at the end of the month and not before
3. Checks arrive within 3 weeks as a postcard
4. Price match prescriptions
5. Purchase +UP reward items FIRST, then use +UP rewards to pay for SCR back items. OOP expense will be less.
6. Watch videos on site for video value coupons to print

Turning Needs Into Freebies…..

Every week you will have needed items you must purchase. Your goal should be to find items to decrease the overall cost if not completely pay for your needed items. This is relatively easy to do using drug store reward programs.

1. Locate items with high reward's back (RR, ECB, +UP)
2. Pay for these items first
3. Use the reward to pay for your needed item

Rolling Rewards For Minimal Cost……

Let's take a look at a few examples of how to get the most for your money at each of these drug stores.

WALGREEN'S:

Purchase # 1—

(1)Stayfree Pads	$1 coupon	$2.99 RR back	$2.99 cost	$1.99 OOP after coupon
(1) Skintimate	$.55 coupon	$2.99 RR back	$2.99 cost	$2.44 OOP after coupon
(1) Tone		$3 RR back	$3.99 cost	$3.99 OOP

TOTAL RR RECEIVED: $8.98 (2) $2.99 + $3

TOTAL OOP: $8.42

COUPONS USED: 2   ITEMS PURCHASED: 3

Purchase # 2—

| (4) Fructis | (4) $4 coupon | $4 RR back | $3.50 cost ea | $ 10/4 OOP |
| (3) Carmels | | | $.33 ea | $.99 OOP |

TOTAL RR RECEIVED: $4

TOTAL RR USED: $8.98 (2) $2.99 & (1)$3

TOTAL OOP: $2.01

COUPONS USED: 7   ITEMS PURCHASED:7

CVS:

Purchase #1—

| (1)Allegra | $2 coupon | $6.99 ECB back | $6.99 cost | $4.99 OOP after coupon |

TOTAL ECB RECEIVED: $6.99

TOTAL OOP: $4.99

Purchase #2---

| (4)Pledge | (2) BOGO coup | $4/$12 ECB back | $3 cost ea | $6/4 OOP after coupon |
| Colgate | $1.50 coupon | $2 ECB back | $2.99 cost | $1.49 OOP after coupon |

TOTAL ECB RECEIVED: $6

TOTAL ECB USED: $6.99

TOTAL OOP: $.50

RITE AID:

Purchase # 1---

| (2)Resolve | (2) $.75 coupon | (2) $1 UP back | $1.99 cost | $1.24 OOP after coupon |
| Listerine | $.50 coupon | $2 UP back | $2.99 cost | $2.49 OOP after coupon |

(2)Stayfree	B1G1 coup + $1	$1.49/2 UP back	$2.49 cost	$1.49 OOP after coupon
Johnson's	$1 manuf & $1 RC	$1 UP back	$2.99 cost	$.99 OOP after coupon

TOTAL UP RECEIVED: $6.49

TOTAL OOP: $7.45

Purchase # 2---

(4)Axe	(2) B1G1	$5/$15 UP back	2/$9cost	(4) $9 after coupon
Bandaids	$.50 manu & $.50 RC		$1.99 cost	$.99 OOP after coupon

TOTAL UP RECEIVED: $5

TOTAL UP USED: $6.49 & $3/15 COUPON

TOTAL OOP: $.50

Once again remember to take your time doing deals at the drug stores. Start with 1 and build up as you gain experience to fill your house with abundant treasures.

"By wisdom a house is built, and by understanding it is established; and by knowledge the rooms are filled with all precious and pleasant riches."

Proverbs 24:3-4

WISDOM BUILDS A HOUSE THROUGH GOOD JUDGEMENT

UNDERSTANDING MAKES IT STRONG

KNOWLEDGE APPLIES WISDOM FOR SUCCESS!

MY LOCAL WALGREEN'S RESTRICTIONS:

- _____
- _____
- _____
- _____

MY LOCAL CVS RESTRICTIONS:

- _____
- _____
- _____
- _____

MY LOCAL RITE AID RESTRICTIONS:

- _____
- _____
- _____
- _____

PART 4 REVIEW

"DRUG STORE DEALING"

DRUG STORE REWARD MATCH UP!

Directions: Put RR (Walgreen's), ECB (CVS), SCR (Rite Aid), or UP (Rite Aid) in the appropriate blank

_____ Expire in 2 weeks from date issued usually

_____ Print out separately from the receipt

_____ Expire 4 weeks from the date issued usually

_____ A check that can be issued at the end of the month for participating purchases

_____ Cannot be used to purchase another of the same item reward received for

_____ Rain checks are issued on out of stock items for these types

_____ "

_____ "

_____ Will be issued after the rebate period if a rain check had to be issued

_____ Count like a coupon

_____ Limit the number you can buy for these items as stated in ad

_____Limit of 4 per person per item

_____ 2% received quarterly based on purchases

_____ Arrive in 3 weeks as a postcard

_____ Will usually need a filler when using these

_____ Should be logged in on website after purchase to receive

HOW DID YOU DO?

RR-RR-ECB-SCR-RR-ECB-UP-SCR-SCR-RR-ECB-UP-ECB-SCR-RR-SCR

PART 5

COUPONING TO CHANGE YOUR LIFE

REDUCING DEBT THROUGH COUPONING

BUILDING A FOOD BANK

SUMMING IT ALL UP

Reducing Debt Through Couponing.....

One of the greatest challenges facing families today is that of increased debt. Many are struggling to pay their bills and make ends meet. The economy has played a big part in this as it has left many people facing unemployment. Not only does this create financial stress upon families, but also creates emotional and relational stress upon its members. Unfortunately many families do not survive this challenge as a team effort and families are often dissolved as the bills mount up. We have virtually 2 choices as we are unexpectedly hit with these challenges: become depressed and give up OR find the answers to help us solve our problems. Finding the answers is the only solution that will ever bring the success we desire. Often the answers are found in the simplest of things like couponing. When you begin to apply the principles you have learned in this book you will undoubtedly see at least a 50% decrease in your grocery spending. Many experience as much as a 70% decrease. Think about that for a moment. If you spend $800 a month on groceries and are able to cut this back to $400, you now have an extra $400 to apply to bills, car payments, emergency fund or savings account. That is $4800 a year! It's like getting a bonus. Could you use a bonus like this? Who couldn't!

What we do with our savings determines our real success. A wise saver will understand the importance of using their savings to get completely out of debt and enjoy the freedom that comes with wise living. With debt gone one can be readily available to meet the needs of others that arise as well as enjoy many of the pleasures of life without burdensome debt.

Let's look at 4 key principles to reducing debt:

1. Set goals
    "Where there is no vision the people perish...." Prov 29:18

2. Figure expenses
    "Know WELL the face of your flocks; and pay attention to your herds." Prov 27:23

3. Prepare a budget to meet expenses
    "Which of you intending to build a tower, does not first sit down and count the cost whether he may have enough to finish it." Luke 14:28-29

4. Devise a plan to include savings and emergency funds
    "Strategic planning is the key to warfare..." Prov 24:6

Use Savings to Knock Out Debt

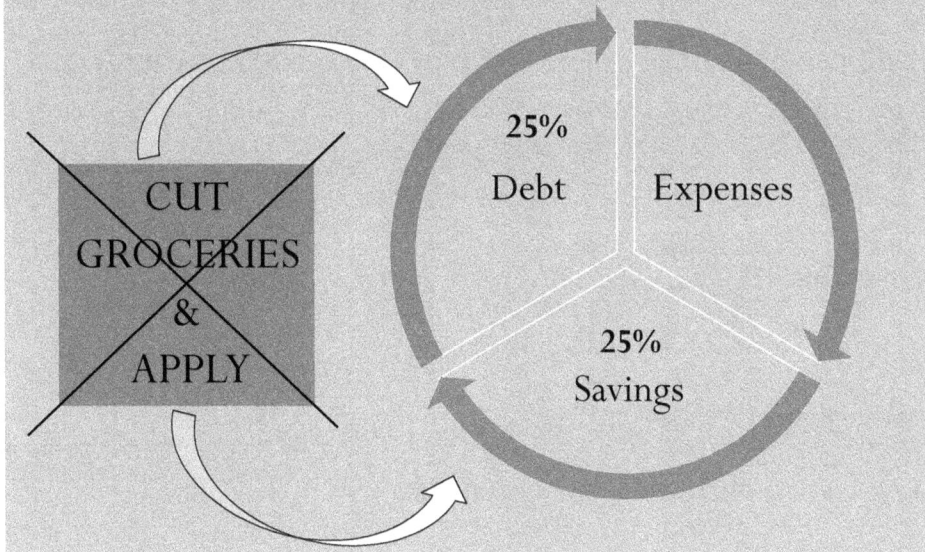

CUT GROCERIES & APPLY

25% Debt   Expenses

25% Savings

SAVE $200 MONTH = $100 SAVED + $100 REDUCED DEBT

TAKE THE PERCENTAGE YOU SAVE ON GROCERIES AND DIVIDE IT BETWEEN DEBT & YOUR SAVINGS AND EMERGENCY FUND.

Always start paying off the smallest debts first. The big ones often seem unreachable and it is easier to start small and work your way up.

BEWARE OF THE MONEY THIEF WHEN YOU START SAVING. The money thief wears many hats and will slyly and easily steal your abundance before you are aware of it if you aren't careful.

Some things that steal your abundance:

1. DON'T use savings to buy extra wants
   "…..each one of you is to put aside and save as he may prosper." 1 Cor 16:2

2. DON'T buy it if you can't pay cash for it (you will need more clothes before you pay for the ones you charged)
   "It is better to not vow than to vow and not pay." Ecc 5:5

3. DON'T use emergency money for non-emergencies
   "…..there he squandered his estate with loose living." Luke 15:13

4. DON'T use this week's assigned money planning to put it back next week. "....the borrower becomes the lender's slave." Prov 22:7

5. DON'T neglect giving thinking you can't afford it---YOU CAN'T AFFORD NOT TO GIVE! "He who is generous will be blessed...." Prov22:9

Building a Food Bank......

STEP #1---Set up a coupon center

      (create 2 binders for nonfood/food items to file

      Coupons brought in.)

STEP # 2---Create weekly give lists around sale items + coupons

STEP # 3---Have a savings contest or goal oriented activity (one

      who brings in the most for the least OOP expense

      wins a prize) Assign by classes

SAMPLE YEARLY FOOD BANK PLAN....

January	February	March	April
Paper towels	Diapers	Dish soap	Shampoo
Toilet paper	Wipes	Cleaning	Soap
Kleenex	Feminine	Sponges	Toothpaste
Can Fruit	Boxed Food	Condiments	Lotion
Can Vegetables	Boxed Desserts	Sugar	Deodorant
Canned Meat	Peanut Butter	Flour	Juices
Ziploc Bags	Jello	Salt	Can Drinks
Alum foil	Pudding	Pepper	Kool-aid
	Popcorn	Cooking Spray	

This will help you create a well balanced supply of ongoing items to your food bank.

STEP 2 TO ABUNDANCE : Giving!!!!

"Give and it shall be given unto you." Luke 6:38

Obviously if we receive through giving we probably lack through not giving. We must understand that sometimes what doesn't make much sense is the very thing that will build your abundance. We don't have to explain everything, we just have to trust God's word to be true.

Some ways we can give:

1. Give to the military stationed overseas
   (They can use expired coupons 6 month's past the expiration date)
   Mail to : Kristi Seigrist, Family Services Coordiantor, 48 FSS/FSFR, Unit S200, Box 105, APO, AE 09461

2. Give what you want to increase in your home
   "The earth brought forth vegetation and plants yielding seed according to their own kind…." Gen 1:12
   (If you need food, give food, if you need money give money, if you need coupons give some away, etc…)

Summing It All Up……

"….You can have abundance so you will be furnished in abundance for every good work."

2 Cor 9:8

The Abundant Believer will----

----Believe God gives the ability to achieve

----Introduce their hands to their belief

----Cause their hands to reach out to others

----Open their hands to receive the blessings

For with God ALL things are possible. God is the Alpha and Omega, the beginning and the end, which is, which was, and which is to come, the Almighty. (Rev. 1:8)

My Food Bank Plan:

- _____
- _____
- _____
- _____
- _____
- _____
- _____
- _____
- _____
- _____
- _____
- _____
- _____
- _____
- _____

My Budget:

Monthly Expenses:

(Include tithe, food, clothing, gas, power, water, phone, car or house payment, etc….-any expenses you acquire on a monthly basis)

_____   _____

_____   _____

_____   _____

_____   _____

_____   _____

_____   _____

_____   _____

_____   _____

TOTAL:

Outstanding debts:

(Include doctor bills, credit cards, school loans, etc….-any that add a burden to your finances that seem hard to stay on top of)

_____   _____

_____   _____

_____   _____

_____   _____

_____   _____

_____   _____

TOTAL:

PROJECTED SAVINGS AMOUNT ON GROCERIES:

**% TO PUT IN SAVINGS ACCOUNT:

**% TO PAY ON DEBT:

**% TO PUT IN AN EMERGENCY FUND:

% TO PUT IN A VACATION FUND:

% TO PUT IN A CHRISTMAS FUND:

You may not start out dividing up into all these categories, however as your debt decreases you should put a percentage back in all of these categories. I have starred the most important ones to start with.

Remember tithe is not an option it is God's money. If we want to prosper we MUST tithe.

"Bring the whole tithe into the storehouse, so that there may be food in My house, and test Me now in this," says the Lord of hosts, "if I will not open for you the windows of heaven and pour out for you a blessing until it overflows?" Malachi 3:8-10

"Honor the Lord from your wealth and from the first of all your produce; so your barns will be filled with plenty and your vats will overflow with new wine." Prov 3:9-10

PART 5 REVIEW

"COUPONING TO CHANGE YOUR LIFE"

SCRIPTURE MATCH UP!

Directions: Match the correct scripture with the statement it best fits.

A. "Where there is no vision the people perish...." Prov 29:18
B. "Know WELL the face of your flocks; and pay attention to your herds." Prov 27:23
C. "Which of you intending to build a tower, does not first sit down and count the cost whether he may have enough to finish it." Luke 14:28-29
D. "Strategic planning is the key to warfare..." Prov 24:6
E. ".....each one of you is to put aside and save as he may prosper." 1 Cor 16:2
F. "It is better to not vow than to vow and not pay." Ecc 5:5
G. ".....there he squandered his estate with loose living." Luke 15:13
H. "....the borrower becomes the lender's slave." Prov 22:7
I. "He who is generous will be blessed...." Prov22:9
J. "The earth brought forth vegetation and plants yielding seed according to their own kind...." Gen 1:12

1. Give what you want to increase in your home _____

2. Prepare a budget to meet expenses _____

3. Devise a plan to include savings and emergency funds _____

4. DON'T buy it if you can't pay cash for it (you will need more clothes before you pay for the ones you charged) _____

5. Figure expenses _____

6. Set goals _____

7. DON'T use emergency money for non-emergencies _____

8. DON'T neglect giving thinking you can't afford it---YOU CAN'T AFFORD NOT TO GIVE! _____

9. DON'T use savings to buy extra wants _____

10. DON'T use this week's assigned money planning to put it back next week. _____

HOW DID YOU DO?

Answer Key:

1. J   2. C   3. D   4. F   5. B   6. A   7. G   8. I   9. E   10. H

NOTES

www.ingramcontent.com/pod-product-compliance
Lightning Source LLC
Chambersburg PA
CBHW051352200326

41521CB00014B/2551